3

In 1983 there were floods. His livestock all died. Even his house was washed away by the floods. His family became very poor. Sour milk and bread were scarce.

Translated from the original *isiZulu*
by Cedric Xulu

N   S
7 0 0 0 0 0 0 0 1 1 3 9 6 9

Mahlase was a well-respected man in Nkandla. He had many goats and cattle.

Mahlase said to his wife, "MaNgobese, tomorrow I am going to look for work. We are all suffering from hunger. My children are very poor."

"But where are you going to go, Baba?" asked MaNgobese.

"They say there are jobs in Durban," replied Mahlase.

Mahlase stood up, took his stick and left the house. Then he went outside and cried. He thought of the old days when he was rich.

Mahlase told everyone he was going. He started collecting his belongings. MaNgobese prepared provisions for him. She killed the last rooster for him. The children ate the heart, legs and head.

Mahlase woke up very early the next morning to catch the bus to Durban. When he arrived in Durban he slept at the railway station.

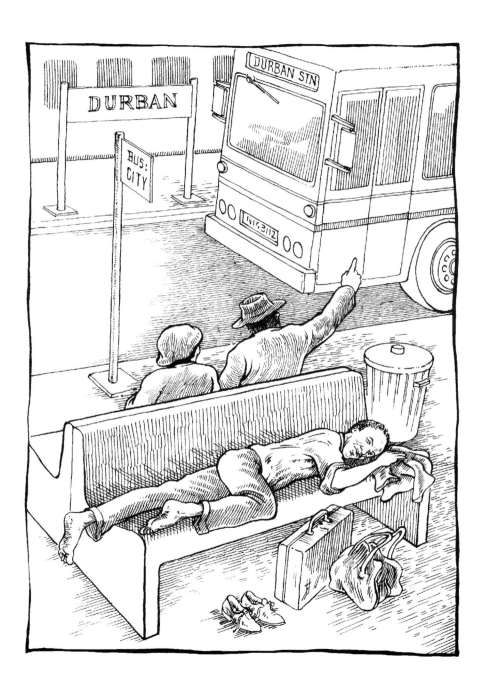

The next morning Mahlase walked around Durban looking for work. Unfortunately, he did not get a job. He then went back to the railway station. He slept there all night.

On the second day, there were many things that troubled him. Firstly, he had finished his provisions. Secondly, the weather was very cold. Thirdly, the railway police chased him away from where he slept.

17

On the third day Mahlase went to look for a job again. He walked as far as the harbour where he saw many people. There was the delicious smell of meat. He thought only of one thing – a traditional feast. He was so hungry, he went straight to the door.

19

Mahlase gave the traditional greeting, saying loudly, "I greet you all in the house." He repeated his greeting three times. At last he realised that no-one could hear him.

He went closer and repeated the greeting, "I greet you all in the house." Still no-one answered him. He took off his hat and entered the house.

"We welcome you to the Wimpy, Baba. Come and sit here. Can I give you something to drink while you wait?" asked a beautiful young woman.

"My daughter, could you take me to the men?" asked Mahlase.

"No, Baba, you can sit here. We will give you anything you want. We have chicken, beef and mutton. What will you have?" she asked.

Mahlase thanked her heartily because he was so hungry. He asked for beef and a beer.

The young lady gave him cold beer and wrote something on a piece of paper. Before he finished his beer she came back with the beef.

When Mahlase finished eating he called the woman back. "My daughter I thank you. I would like you to call the head of this household so that I can thank him. Where I come from we don't eat and just disappear without thanking the host."

The waitress was confused. Then she realised that Mahlase did not know what to do. She explained what had happened to the manager of the restaurant.

The manager spoke to Mahlase. "Baba, do you have a problem?" he asked.

"No, my son, I would like to thank you very much," said Mahlase with a smile. "I have enjoyed your food and I would like to leave now."

The manager kept quiet. He tried to think of what to say. He realised that this man was not a crook. However, he also realised that a lot of money had been wasted.

"Baba, would you like to work here? You can work for two months. After that, we will see if we can give you a permanent job," he said.

Mahlase was overjoyed. He sang the manager's praises. People stood and looked at him. "I wonder what MaNgobese will say when I tell her about this!" Mahlase shouted joyfully.

THE END

Thanks

We thank the following people for their help in evaluating the original *isiZulu* version of this story:

Nkosinathi Ngcobo, Jabu Ngiba, Beatrice Mabaso, Philile Dhlamini, Mandy Macebo, Kay Ntshangase, Wendy Vimba, Zanele Mabaso and Thabo Kubheka.

We thank the following people for their help in evaluating the English version of this story:

Shelley Seid (facilitator), Emily Dladla, Constance Mthembu, Dudu Laza, Armstrong Nkomo, Jabulile Sibisi and Xoliswa Hulley from the University of Natal Adult Literacy Programme.

NEW READERS PUBLISHERS

New Readers Publishers is a non-profit publishing project based in the School of Community Development and Adult Learning at the University of Natal in Durban. The aim of the project is to contribute to an increase in adult literacy and the promotion of a reading culture. It does this by developing and publishing easy readers in all of South Africa's official languages and by increasing the capacity of teachers through training. The books are read for education and entertainment in first or additional languages.

New Readers Publishers is supported by Rockefeller Brothers Fund.

How to contact us

If you want to find out more about New Readers Publishers or about other books that we publish, please contact:

New Readers Publishers
School of Community Development and Adult Learning
University of Natal
Durban
4041
Tel: 031 – 2602568
Fax: 031 – 2601168
E-mail: keyser@nu.ac.za
Website: www.nrp.und.ac.za

Mahlase's feast

English version first published 2002 by
New Readers Publishers
School of Community Development and Adult Learning
University of Natal, Durban 4041
South Africa

Translated from **uMahlase uvakashela edolobheni** (*isiZulu*)

Copyright © New Readers Publishers

Cover illustration by Jeff Rankin
Design and desktop publication by Lesley Lewis of Inkspots, Durban
Printed by Interpak Books, Pietermaritzburg

ISBN: 1-86840-487-0